THE STRUGGLE FOR SOY

*And Other Dilemmas
of a Korean Adoptee*

MEGAN SOUND

S

ISBN 978-0-692-04918-1

For adoptees, dreamers, wonderers and wanderers, and a world that will allow Helen Lou to reach her full potential.

CONTENTS

1 Go Home! 1

2 The Struggle for Soy 11

3 Knock, Knock. Who's There? 19

4 Can I Get a 'Ching Chong'? 31

5 Small Talk 39

6 Guessing Games 47

7 Gag Me With a Chopstick 53

8 Touching the Void 59

9 Name Changer 75

10 To Breed, or Not to Breed 81

11 Message in a Bottle to My Birth Mom 91

Acknowledgments 103

GO HOME!

MY PARENTS ACTED ON MY BEHALF to make me a citizen. Had they not jumped through the legal hoops when they first got me, I'd be at risk of deportation to a country I've never included on the list of places that come to mind when strangers have yelled at me, "Go back to where you came from!"

When I heard about Korean adoptee Adam Crasper's deportation in 2016, it made me stop and consider my own comfort as a citizen who "belongs here." Like me, Adam was adopted from South Korea. That might be the only thing our stories have in common. Adam has described his first set of adoptive parents as evangelistic Christians who "incorporated a lot of corporal punishment into their discipline." When Adam was nine, those parents decided they no longer wanted him or his (biological) sister. They were separated and placed in foster homes. Adam eventually ended up in Oregon, with adoptive parents Thomas and Dolly Crasper. Not much of an improvement from his first set of adoptive parents, as the Craspers were abusive. *The New York Times* published an article that noted, "The state ultimately did charge the couple with dozens of counts of child abuse, including rape, sexual abuse and criminal mistreatment; they were convicted in 1992 on several counts of criminal mistreatment and assault, and (the father) was convicted on one count of sexual abuse, though he served just 90 days in prison." Adam lived with the Craspers until he was 16, when he was thrown out. He later went back to break in, to retrieve the rubber shoes and Korean Bible that he traveled to the U.S. with when he was a baby. He was arrested and spent more than two years in jail. More charges followed in the years to come: misdemeanors, assault, unlawful firearms possession. None of his adoptive parents ever completed the process to make him a citizen, so when he applied for a green card through the Department of Homeland Security in 2012, his criminal history set the deportation process in motion. He was deported to South Korea at the age of 41, a country he left 38 years earlier.

There are an estimated 35,000 international adoptees living in the United States who don't have citizenship. These are adult adoptees who were born before February 27, 1983; the 2001 law that gives automatic citizenship to adoptees from other countries does not cover them. I imagine the reality of being deported is terrifying for these individuals —at least the ones who are aware of their citizenship status, or lack thereof.

I was given a small American flag on the day I was naturalized as a U.S. citizen. I was three. I remember holding that flag, rolling the staff between my fingers so the stars and stripes waved in front of me, as much as the cheap, stiff material they were on would allow. If I didn't have a picture of me in the St. Louis courthouse from that day, American flag in hand, I'd be worried about the possibility of deportation. Even with the assurance that my parents went through the proper channels to get me citizenship, the seed of doubt inside is watered when I hear about the possibility of clerical errors or oversights. United States law is literally making adoptees go back to where they came from.

I've been keenly aware of the volatile line between inclusion and exclusion my entire life. In elementary school having the same stuff as others admitted one to the group: perm, Keds, Swatch Watch, Umbros—on occasion I rocked all that at once (thanks 80s fashion!). Junior High was more of the same, plus avoiding being the subject of rumors and gossip (To this day I wonder who started the rumor of catching [a kid who shall not be called out by name] masturbating in the boy's bathroom. Hindsight tells me it was some insecure popular kid abusing their social status, to ruin the reputation and remaining school days of [the kid].) Fitting in in high school, or at least feeling like I did, meant sticking with the group of artsy/musical/Patagonia jacket wearing people who I gravitated toward, and being friendly with the athletes (aka popular group), as a measure of safety, because I saw how they were valued more than other groups of students by our school's administration.

I actually enjoyed being on the softball and lacrosse teams. I even had a letter jacket. I was proud to have my own "girls" style rather than wear some guy's. Letter jackets (are they still a thing?!) were an expression of being part of something *and* an individual. The letters sewn on the chest of the jacket were a reminder of the team or club the wearer belongs to, and the jacket owner's name was embroidered on the front, or in the case of my "girls" letter jacket, displayed via a triple layered felt patch on the back. It's as if the jacket says, "This person belongs to something bigger than their self, but they haven't lost their name." At least that's the spiel mine spun for me.

Inclusion and the spaces that are able to make us feel so became an obsession of mine when I began drinking coffee at age 27. Coffee served me freedom like a driver's license and a set of wheels serves a teenager. Coffee fueled my curiosity. I was driven to folklore that involves dancing goats and delivered to third places, starting with *The Great Good Place.*

Written by sociologist Ray Oldenburg, *The Great Good Place* explores the essence of third places —"a setting beyond home and work (the 'first' and second' places) in which people relax in good company and do so on a regular basis." Think *Cheers.* The opening credit song for that television show captured the spirit of how a true third place makes you feel: understood, relaxed, protected from the noise, and like you belong.

Making your way in the world today takes everything you've got.
Taking a break from all your worries, sure would help a lot.
Wouldn't you like to get away?
Sometimes you want to go

where everybody knows your name,
and they're always glad you came.
You wanna be where you can see,
our troubles are all the same
You wanna be where everybody knows
Your name.

If *Cheers* is the TV representation of a third place, then coffee shops are the real deal. That is, small scale, independently owned ones. The kind that *feel* like they have a soul and are an extension of the caring owner who runs them. These types of places are becoming harder to find, buried (and unfortunately sometimes crushed) by entities whose priority is profit, not building and maintaining relationships. Not yet fully awake to this realization, I visited coffee shops in the U.S., Canada, UK, Ireland, France, and Italy; I was on a coffee driven quest to understand what it takes for a place to make you feel included. I found my favorite third place in Eureka, California.

Has Beans feels like a welcoming place. Large windows let light in and allow patrons to see the bay full of boats, a live plant hangs in the opposite bay window where an upright bass lays on its side above. Six large tapestries billow from the ceiling and a coffee mug with the chemical makeup of caffeine sits on the counter with pens in it. Smokey

Robinson's voice pours out of the speakers, then Otis Redding's, followed by Led Zeppelin and Rod Stewart. The barista exudes kindness and doesn't flinch when one patron pays for their house coffee with all change. Her friendly vibe fills the space, as does her voice when she casually explains what an Americano is to a woman at the counter who's having trouble deciding what to order. Everyone is made to feel welcome, including an elderly woman who arrives carrying a stuffed animal duck in her gold sequin bag. Not an ounce of judgement or agitation is expressed by the barista or the owner, who quietly and gently leads a loud, belligerent local outside—I'm guessing to explain why their proposal of, "I'll go away for a shot of coffee," won't work. The coffee shop owner seems to have limitless patience and diffuses early signs of edginess before they become contagious. Even as a one time visitor, I'm a recipient of the genuine spirit that's shared in this space.

I ran into the complete opposite vibe in Deuville, France. Coffee, curiosity, and Couchsurfing led me to the posh beach town where the American Film Festival happened to be taking place when I was there. At the festival coffee tent I was offered a cappuccino that sat unclaimed on the counter for who knows how long. I declined and ordered a macchiato instead; I was shamed by the barista's eye scan of me, reluctantly served, then dismissed when they turned to stand with their back to me. I headed to the red carpet where John Reilly was walking past the crowd, some of who were asking for autographs. When it became apparent he wasn't going to give any, one guy yelled, "Go home!"

We're at the *American* Film Festival, Jay Z's ode to NYC "Empire State of Mind" is blasting through the speakers, and this Frenchman is hurling vitriol at John Reilly. I feel disoriented to witness the demand of "Go home!" directed at a white man. I am so used to being the one who's told to leave, or watching other Asian and Middle Eastern people told the same thing. The Frenchman flipped the script and I realize how it's all connected: welcomeness.

"Go home" and all its iterations basically translate to "Get away from me." It reminds me of toddlers, mid-tantrum, screaming, "I hate you! I want [name of other parent/any alternative caretaker/favorite stuffed animal]!" In the Frenchman's case, he decided he hated John Reilly because Reilly didn't give him an autograph.

Insecurity and entitlement have a funny way of getting tangled together. From lawn chairs and orange cones staking claim on parking spots in cities to land claims throughout the history of the United States, it all seems to be rooted in the same desire to have a designated place where one belongs —the varying factor being the level of harm done to others in exchange for one's own security.

President Trump's executive order that blocked immigration from seven countries and halted refugees from Syria came 36 years (almost exactly to the day) after my own arrival to the U.S. A person who makes a choice to ban refugees does not see the full humanity of those affected and does not feel empathy for their fellow earth-dwelling neighbors. They draw lines and wish to build walls to reinforce those lines that divide. They lack a feeling of belonging despite the towers they've bought and the fame they've acquired, so they do all they can to strip others of feeling welcome in their own bodies and across borders. Tragically, they don't realize their own sense of belonging could be cultivated if they started replacing "Go Home!" with "Welcome." The same is true for all of us.

THE STRUGGLE FOR SOY

THE "ASIAN FOODS" SIGN that hangs above the aisle simultaneously establishes a grocery store ghetto (*hey people whose ethnicity is Asian, stay in THIS area*) and reminds me that the label of Asian is affixed to me, too. My body tenses when I enter the vicinity of rice noodles and water chestnuts. I'm reduced to feeling less like a multifaceted human and more like a thing that falls into the same category as cans of La Choy products. Small cans of mandarin oranges await being added to any salad to make it definitively *Asian.* I quickly scan the shelves for what I need and see a single soy sauce bottle on the top shelf, just out of reach.

I completely understand the compulsion to label. I find a sense of relief and ease after categorizing and labeling, my brain relaxes after it neatly organizes or understands—and because my brain is lazy like most human brains, it would be very content to just kick back and let labels be labels. When I was a kid, I took labeling literally. I had an embossing label maker that I used to mark all of the office supplies I used. I played office because it seemed more interesting to me than playing house. My stapler had "STAPLER," stamped on it, my box of paper clips were labeled "PAPER CLIPS," and my desktop tape dispenser read, "TAPE." These were gratuitous labels, unlike the much needed labels I encountered later in life that helped me learn Spanish in Señora Walker's class. Libraries and grandmothers were tagged "biblioteca" and "abuela" in the cartoon collages of my Spanish textbook. Flashcards were full of labels for me to learn: contento, triste, asi asi; mujer, hombre, niño.

I like that labels help me get my bearing, but settling with them as a destination seems like my lazy brain at play. Only now do I wonder how I might have limited those supplies I had as a kid by placing labels on them. Even the term SUPPLIES seems restrictive. What if my paper clips longed to be art? I squelched their full potential. I can empathize with them, I've felt limited by labels too.

The label I abhorred during my entire childhood and adolescence was the most visibly obvious: Asian. I was not interested in being Asian, at all. My mom was white, my dad was white, my brother was white, and later, my "half" brothers were white—because my stepmom was white too. I wanted to fit in with them, which was an impossibility when it came to my appearance. As a person of color in America, one of the first covert lessons I learned is that white is right; white is beautiful, as was evidenced by all the white faces I saw in my *Seventeen* magazines growing up; white is talented, as is evidenced by the roles of Asian characters in Hollywood given to white actors; white is influential, as is evidenced by CEOs, late night television, and 44/45 U.S. Presidents. My logic seemed sound: *If* you have to be white to be beautiful, talented, or influential, *then* my non-white self is flawed.

My solution was to spite Asian stereotypes. I didn't take as many photographs with my Canon as I would have liked. I was afraid of looking like one of those Asian tourists I saw mocked in countless Hollywood flicks. Excelling at math was not something I worried about, my "C" in calculus came naturally. I resisted the silent Asian woman archetype at my first real job after graduating from college by communicating directly and with force. When we all went out drinking together, it wasn't unusual for me to take a swing at someone with fist or chair—anger was a natural byproduct of denying myself the convenience of being me.

Being labeled Asian was inevitable (after all, my ethnicity is Korean); I grew used to seeing myself in the same vein as people who I heard say, "You all look alike." To me, this perception of likeness stripped away my individuality and swept me into the silent sea of Asians, so when a guy I was dating in college told me, "I've never met anyone like you," I assumed it was just a line rather than an invitation. He'd just presented the door to belonging, a place where I'd be accepted because of who I was rather than how well I fit in to a role— and, being the gentleman that he was, opened it wide for me. I refused to cross the threshold. I didn't even take a single step toward it. Instead of hearing the sincerity and admiration in his tone that suggested he saw multitudes in me, I questioned the compliment until it landed like a criticism. *I've never met someone who looks Asian but acts so white.* I was painfully incapable of accepting that guy's fondness for the complete version of me.

In a parallel universe, maybe more men I dated made me feel like I belonged by simply being me, but in this life it took another decade before I found and married a man who didn't get caught up in seeing only the labels affixed to me. Actually being seen is powerful. It feels so different than simply being looked at. Without the fear of being seen as a stereotype, I started to explore the Asian aspect of myself. In order to learn about my Korean heritage, I read kids books. Square one was where I had to begin. Flipping through smooth pages filled with vibrant photos of Korea's varied landscape, I learned about the Korean peninsula. The oversized print told me that the Korean language borrows many words from the Chinese language. Under a bright red "Pastimes" subtitle, the book spoke directly to me, "South Koreans love to have fun. They like such sports as soccer, basketball, baseball, and tennis. They also like to go to concerts, plays, and movies, just as you do." How'd the book know I like to go to plays and movies?! For the first time, I confidently thought to myself, *I'm Korean. I'm a Korean adoptee. I'm an Asian American.*

The grocery store I frequent keeps soy sauce on the top shelf in the Asian foods area. I'm 5'3"; I can comfortably reach something that's at the front of the top shelf—anything beyond that is a stretch. I find myself standing on the bottom shelf for extra leverage and holding on to the lip of the top shelf with one hand, reaching for the single bottle of soy sauce at the very back of the shelf. I feel predictable and ridiculous. I imagine the people walking by behind me slowing their roll to stare and see the Asian reach for the soy sauce like it's liquid gold. The tip of my middle finger touches the surface of the bottle, and the soy sauce slowly rotates, turning away from me like I've turned away from my Asian identity for years.

I step down from the shelf. Deep breath. *How bad do I want the soy sauce?* No worker is around to lend a hand, if I want the sauce I have to get it myself. I step on the bottom shelf again, grab hold of the top shelf with my left hand, reach back toward the bottle with my right. The bottle teases me as it turns and turns from my touch—one final complete body stretch from tippy toes to fingertips and I seize the soy. I SEIZE THE SOY.

This soy sauce is better than liquid gold. And to think of all the times I needed soy sauce and just kept walking by if it looked like it might be slightly out of reach. The battle was strictly internal. *What if people see me reaching for it and I don't get it? What if they see me struggling and don't offer to help? What if they laugh at me because all they see is AN ASIAN SOY SAUCE ADDICT?*

When people ask me if I speak a language besides English, sometimes I tell them yes, if I'm feeling playful. "Oh yeah? What language?" They ask, expecting me to respond, "Chinese," "Japanese," or maybe even "Korean."

"Spanish," I tell them. "Un poquito." I can only conjugate a few verbs and talk pencils, boogers, and bathrooms, but I count that as knowing at least a little. Enough to say:

Yo soy yo.

KNOCK, KNOCK. WHO'S THERE?

WHEN I MET MARGARET CHO in 2008, all I could do was cry. A group of about 20 of us were led backstage through a narrow hallway to meet her after her Denver performance at the Paramount Theater. Standing in line, I was surprised at how nervous I felt. There was a tremble in my voice even as I imagined what I wanted to say to Margaret when it was my turn to meet her. To see her flip the script on racist people and stereotypes during her stand-up set, to hear her say, "I think it's very important to feel beautiful, I think it's very political to feel beautiful," affirmed desires I carried but hesitated to acknowledge.

Feeling beautiful seemed off limits to me when I was growing up. It would have required that I resemble, even remotely, the faces I saw in magazines and on screen. I watched countless movies during my childhood and early adolescence, oblivious to what all of them were missing. My 10 favorite films from the 80s:

1. Annie (1982)
2. Ghostbusters (1984)
3. Sixteen Candles (1984)
4. The Breakfast Club (1985)
5. The Goonies (1985)
6. Pee-Wee's Big Adventure (1985)
7. Back to the Future (1985)
8. Ferris Bueller's Day Off (1986)
9. Big (1988)
10. Beetlejuice (1988)

As Phoebe Robinson would say, these movies are full of "Sooo many white guys." And white gals. The ten most influential films of my formative years and only two of them feature an Asian actor. None of them showed me what it looks like when an Asian American girl is part of the story. Rather, watching them made me accept invisibility. Maybe things would have been different if I watched independent films or if I didn't live in a suburb in the Midwest. "Maybe" isn't a territory I messed with much. It's a slippery slope for most adoptees. I tended to stay in my "It's all I know" lane, particularly when people shared their thoughts about my adoptee status. *Gosh it must be so weird to not know your **real** parents! It's so crazy that you're Asian but your family is all white!* I told people, "It's all I know."

***

I'm keenly aware of how laughter can turn on you. When the crowd is laughing at blond jokes I'm wondering how long until ching chong bing bong is dragged into the mix. If laughter is directed at inanimate objects, it just feels safer. To a certain degree, high school felt like four years of being tested for my deflection skills. How many scenarios could I shift laughter from being at the expense of people to being aimed at the sad state of my public school's lunch meat or the latest rigid rule instated by our school's administration? I was like one of those people at the airport who marshal planes to gates using those bright orange light saber stubs. Except instead of directing planes, I directed laughter. I wasn't bad at it for the most part, but then one day I crashed a plane straightaway into a friend.

A group of us were sitting at a table during lunch and Jack Mack (fake name) was in the middle of one of his tirades about how much he hated Jill Johnson (fake name). I never fully understood their relationship. I think they dated at some point. They publicly yelled at each other, most memorably Jack would bark at Jill and Jill would (understandably) get upset and either charge at Jack or storm off, crying.

Jack paused mid-tirade and my staring off into space to avoid participating in his latest poll was not working. "Well?" he asked me. I understood the gist of what was happening and that raising my hand meant agreeing with him and whatever iteration of "Jill is annoying" he was pushing. Everybody around me was raising a hand. It reminded me of the Sure Deodorant commercials ("Raise your hand if you're sure!); I shot my hand in the air, sniffed at my armpit and said, "I'm sure!" Everyone laughed, but my betrayal of Jill immediately made me feel like I was only a shell of myself.

I don't know anyone who enjoys being laughed at. Some people might not care, easily brushing off jokes at their expense from the armor they don. But what happens if you're not the type who moves through the world fully guarded? Also, armor can be pierced. One hole at a time over a span of decades makes for a swiss cheese psyche.

Sixteen Candles punctured my ability to see myself as an Asian American and in a positive light, every time I watched the copy I owned on VHS. Even though I imagined myself as Samantha, it was impossible for me to ignore Long Duk Dong. This is what happens when you're Asian and you don't often see someone who looks like you (similar, not indistinguishable—what are you, racist?) in movies. When you do, it's a big deal. Officially called "representation," the lack of it leaves one feeling invisible and worthless. The double bind comes when Asian characters show up in movies (yay representation), always as the butt of a joke or perpetuating a stereotype (boo misrepresentation). I laughed at Long Duk Dong when I watched *Sixteen Candles* with my friends because not laughing felt like drawing a line and standing on the wrong side of it.

An iconic coming of age story, *Sixteen Candles* is chock-full of humor that hasn't aged well. Today, it's understood that a passed out prom queen can't give consent. In the movie, her boyfriend hands her off to "The Geek" so he can have sex with her. When "The Geek" expresses concern, "I'm only a freshman," her boyfriend replies, "She's so blitzed she won't know the difference." This exchange didn't raise a red flag for me back then. It sank in to my subconscious as acceptable, as did the "bizarre Chinaman" trope delivered by Long Duk Dong, from his first appearance in the film (proceeded by a gong sound) to his last scene in the film, when his accent/less than perfect English is the source of confusion and lots of laughs. "The Donger" isn't the only character we laugh at in the movie, but he is the only Asian. He's described as "the weird Chinese guy," "totally bizarre," and Samantha's younger brother says to "burn the sheets and mattress after he leaves." I watched *Sixteen Candles* dozens of times, each viewing made me want to further alienate myself from the Asian aspect of me.

Everything I knew from movies and television reinforced my desire to be white. My understanding of being Asian meant being laughed at like Long Duk Dong, or playing the role of a gadget loving Asian kid—like Data in *The Goonies*. Every time I witnessed racist jokes in movies or on television, it cost me bits of my self-worth. As much as I didn't want to be Asian American, I was.

I was 14 when *All-American Girl* first aired. Cut from the same cloth as *Rosanne* and *Seinfeld*, it was a sitcom that starred a stand-up comedian. Margaret Cho was 26 at the time, and played a college student who was living at home with her family in San Francisco. Margaret is a Korean American; I didn't realize it at the time, but she was the definitive role model for me when I was a teenager. The show wasn't great—it only lasted one season, but that had nothing to do with how validating it felt to finally see a sitcom that starred an Asian American woman.

There were a lot of terrible shows that survived more than one season. 1994 America wasn't ready for *All-American Girl,* they were busy watching *Full House, Married...with Children, and Home Improvement.* It was about the dominant groups back then: white and black audiences. *Fresh Prince of Bel-Air* managed to reach both, and networks seemed to think they hit their diversity quota with shows like *Martin, Family Matters,* and *Sister,*

Sister. It'd be another decade before Shonda Rhimes's characters would begin normalizing the wide spectrum of marginalized people.

It's getting easier to find stand-up comedians who craft jokes about race at the expense of the racist rather than the minority. This is my preference when it comes to comedy. Like personal taste in the realms of style and reading, sense of humor is free to be forged by each of us, rather than some set of rules that we all agree on: what makes something funny, what definitively defines something as not funny. For a long time, our frame of reference for what was seen as funny was influenced by the people most visibly telling the jokes—a lot of white guys.

One of my favorite comedians is Aziz Ansari. His take on life is different than George Carlin or Steve Martin or Jerry Seinfeld; he's not a white guy. Sure, not all white guys tell the same jokes, but none of them have the experience of living in the United States as a person of color. Aziz has and does, so when I watch one of his specials and see him make his audience question and laugh at racism in a way I've never witnessed before, I rejoice. Absolutely.

He gives a voice to an experience I can relate to, which feels like I myself am being heard.

During one of his comedy specials, Ansari shares how he thinks it's silly when people think racism only happens in places like the south. He goes on to tell a story about his Korean American friend who lives in Los Angeles. His friend got locked out of his apartment so he called a locksmith and when the locksmith asked for his last name and ultimately learned he was talking to a Korean American, he said, "I hate Korean Americans. Korean Americans are trying to destroy America" and hung up on him. Ansari wonders out loud to the audience, "Wow, this guy does no business with Korean Americans? How many Korean Americans would have to call him before economically, he couldn't afford to be that racist? What if Korean people kept calling? Locksmith guy would be like, 'I'd have made $5,000 if I didn't hate Korean people!...Koreans aren't trying to destroy America, they can't even find their keys!" Ansari adds, "But then weirdly, that stereotype would get ingrained into his racism."

Asian American representation in pop culture is and isn't improving. ABC got their successful network primetime television sitcom staring an Asian American family 21 years after *All American Girl* flopped. *Fresh Off the Boat* debuted in 2015; the show is about a Taiwanese American family who moved from Washington, D.C.'s Chinatown to Orlando, Florida to open Cattleman's Ranch, a cowboy themed steak restaurant. The show is set in the 90s and questions white suburban culture in a witty way that flips the script on the "bizarre Chinaman" stereotype. Instead, we get to see how inane certain interests of white people can seem (car racing is mocked during one episode). *Fresh Off the Boat* offers viewers a look at an Asian American family through a frame that's not one of ridicule.

An unreasonable amount of pressure rides on *Fresh Off the Boat*. It's this pressure that causes "Rep sweats"—the anxiety felt about the desire for multifaceted representation of people who look like you in mainstream media. Comedian Jenny Yang is credited with coining the term at a viewing party for the pilot of *Fresh Off the Boat*. She explained, "Asians are so invisible, every time you have the opportunity to see yourself on TV, you hold your breath."

I held my breath for most of my childhood, adolescence, and early adulthood. When I was finally able to exhale, streams of tears accompanied my relief. Margaret Cho didn't seem to mind the salty droplets falling on her shoulder as she hugged me. In fact, she seemed used to it, as if the same scenario had played out hundreds of times in cities across the country.

CAN I GET A 'CHING CHONG'?

I USED TO sit on the plush grey carpet of my family room and watch *Sesame Street* on the regular. And on the regular, it transported me from the spacious suburbs where I lived and was a minority among white people, to urban surroundings where people of color were the norm. I was too young to know how deep the impact of *Sesame Street's* diversity and creative spirit would have on me, but my heart registered it without my brain's knowing—as the heart tends to do.

The cosmos of my imagination began forming during my visits to *Sesame Street* and continued to develop as I encountered creative spirits throughout the years. It eventually came to look something like a collaboration between Jim Henson, Tim Burton, and Michel Gondry. It's a welcoming world with the vibe of Fraggle Rock that's full of characters like Edward Scissorhands, and reveals itself like a surreal music video. I tend to escape to this world when I'm faced with uncomfortable situations; it's where I take breaks from racist/sexist/chauvinist/supremacist realities.

I'm startled but not surprised when people are racist in situations I go into thinking will be free from white supremacism. Like the lecture given by a mycologist that I attended, in which she clearly knew a lot about varieties of mushrooms, but was ignorant to the fact that comparing yellow ones to Asians and red ones to Native Americans was absolutely not okay. Her subtle racism lost its subtly when she went on to explain how sex crazy Asians are, and how they collect certain fungi to be used as an aphrodisiac. She went on to share how "The Asians use big shovels to dig up mushrooms and kill the mycelium."

I got swept away in her generalization and mentally recalled the three other Asians in the audience who I noticed before the talk started. I imagined the four of us with giant shovels, wearing conical hats, wreaking havoc on a hillside of mushrooms, laughing wild Oriental cackles that aren't really a thing, except the "Isms-R-Us" factory in my mind made them one, along with other over the top racist flourishes that I pictured the mycologist stocked up on. Maybe she was a mycologist by day and hoarder of racishes (racist flourishes) when she returned to her home each evening. Perhaps she'd collected so many by this point, when she opened her front door this evening, they'd spill out and surround her, forming a tornado that picked her up and transported her to the Land of Racishes, where she'd have to solve a series of riddles and achieve personal transformation before she could depart by eating a mushroom and waking to a house free of racish clutter.

There's a lot of people who could benefit from a trip to the Land of Racishes, I know this because a handful of them have stopped me on the street. One older man was hanging out the passenger side of a truck, cigarette dangling from his fingers, when he hollered out to me as I was walking down the sidewalk, "Excuse me! I was just betting money that you're Korean."

"Oh yeah?" I answered, calculating how threatened I felt. Zero threatened I decided. It was light out and

I was on a busy street. Plenty of cars around as witnesses, in case this man jumped out of his car and grabbed me, throwing me into the back to take me to a lab to confirm my Koreaness.

"Yeah, somethin' about you is Korean" he explained.

I wondered what it could be. Was it the giant grey hoodie I was wearing? No. That was MADE IN HONDURAS. Was it the straight-leg black sweatpants I was sporting? No. MADE IN INDONESIA. Was it something in the way that I moved? I had to check myself, as my imagination quickly directed what a scene of me skipping down the sidewalk, Gangnam Style would look like. RIDICULOUS.

Knowing our conversation would soon be over once the stoplight turned green, I asked the man, "You bet money?" He seemed tripped up by this. He started to stutter and repeated, "I was just sayin' there's something about you that's Korean." Did he think I was going to demand a cut of the money if I told him I was Korean? Was this wager at the top of the slippery slope to a life of greed gaming for me?

I pictured bobsledding down a track full of twists with this man, reaching my hand out to retrieve Super Mario coins, each one making that most satisfying ba-ding sound as I gathered them. Maybe I'd even end up saving Princess Toadstool and we'd go on to have a harrowing Thelma and Louise adventure. I get the appeal of wanting to escape from your life. At some point, all the small yet significant encounters add up and you find yourself at a point of wanting to just walk away, to claim the act of walking, rather than let it be interpreted as what it is too often— public display of the body.

I was walking to get coffee one morning when I passed a church where there were a couple of guys standing out front. When one of them said "Hello," I said, "Hi" because I feel like responding to greetings is the decent, human thing to do. I hadn't taken three steps past them before I heard one guy say to the other, "That's what I'm going to do. Get me an Asian girl."

I fill with rage even without unpacking the implications of what he just said, but my imagination insists on calming me, because fury is a toxic parasite and holding onto it is like inviting it to feed on your spirit like an all you can eat buffet. My mind drops the guy in the middle of what looks like a Muppet movie from the 80s, and his comment is turned inside out as it leaves the mouth of an enthusiastic, yet misguided Gonzo. He's preparing for a spectacular stunt, the first of its kind in the entire universe—he's going to build a Rube Goldberg machine, completely out of chickens and cantaloupes! Gonzo's all set, except he needs to find a thingamabob to drop into his contraption. It's gotta be shiny. It's gotta be nimble. It's gotta be resilient. Thrilled by his own brilliance, Gonzo exclaims, "THAT'S WHAT I'M GOING TO DO! GET ME AN ASIAN PEARL!" What?! It makes no sense, which is sometimes just what's needed.

***

I was at the youth center where I worked for more than a decade, when one day I was doing my duty of "walking the halls." Our team of staff was expected to all pitch in when it came to disciplining the kids who decided they liked hanging out in the common areas instead of the programmed areas like the art room and technology lab. As I walked past three boys leaning against a painted cinderblock wall that spanned from the gym to the social recreation room, one of them said, "Ching Chong." I paused to turn toward them, and a preacher who looked like Prince in a giant purple Stop Making Sense style suite, materialized in my mind.

D e a r l y B e l o v e d , w e a r e
g a t h e r e d h e r e t o d a y t o g e t
t h r o u g h t h i s t h i n g c a l l e d
l i f e .
Let's dance our cares away let the music play leave our judgement at the door stop keeping score start connecting our heart and our head it's been too long we've gone without listening to the songs of our souls the song of my soul the song of your soul muffled by media distractions consumer contraptions thingy mabobs w h a t c h a m a c a l l i t s happymeals hassle free life hack hijacks your will to survive and thrive to design your own life choose your own adventure l e a p and the net will appear quiet courage underrated 'cause it's overlooked but it's there walking the talk when hollywood heroes are silent night holy night all is not calm but that's alright we're the ones who will click our heels make it happen walkabout different paths different paces so long rat race splinter nothing personal

thank you for your service self serve soft serve fro
yo lo lo yo fro do re mi the sound of music makes
the hills alive t h e   h i l l s   a r e   a l i v e
w i t h   m a g i c   dance magic dance ground
control to major tom is the earth still blue roy gee
roger that

I didn't stop to ask the boys why they said what
they said, or if, as my imagination preferred to play
it, they thought "Ching Chong" is synonymous with
"Amen!" Before walking past them I disciplined
some younger kids running in and out of the
bathroom. Maybe they saw this and approved,
hence throwing a "Ching Chong!" my way. I don't
have the luxury of living in this imaginative realm
all the time, so in this single moment, I'll take it.

SMALL TALK

"I LIKE YOUR CHINESE BANGS. Where you from?" I looked into the big brown eyes of the third grade girl standing before me, her face open, innocent, and completely unaware that her compliment was laced with insult. I restrained myself from bursting into laughter from the sweet absurdity of her question.

I love how having a conversation with a kid can feel like solving a mystery. An eight year old boy once asked me, "Do you make Chinese, er, Japanese birds?" He must have seen my brow furrow while I tried to understand if he thought I was God. He explained, "We made fish today in school, but I want to make a bird." Ahhhh. With just a touch of context, my mind made a connection to what my husband had once told me about the levels of origami difficulty. You start out folding fish, then advance to frogs, birds, and dinosaurs. "Sorry," I told the boy, "I don't know how to do origami." He looked slightly disappointed that I couldn't show him how to fold a bird, but pleased that I didn't ask him, "What in the world are you talking about?" A question that likely flowed frequently from the mouths of adults in his life.

I spent ten years working for a non-profit where my sole responsibility was to make youth feel like they had somewhere they belonged, like they had an adult in their life besides their parents or legal guardians who truly, genuinely, deeply cared for them. My priority at work was to walk with the kids along the twisted line between belonging and individuality. It's no accident that I gravitated toward this type of work; I still had my own navigating to carry out. I looked under the "at risk" label affixed to them by some adults, in order to see their full humanity. What did I find? The joy and wonder that is being a kid. Sure, some of them were already experiencing stress in their lives. Maybe they didn't know when they'd eat their next meal.

Or they would leave the youth center to arrive to a dark home—literally, because their electricity was turned off. Or maybe there was no home of their own, maybe their family lived in a motel room, or no room at all. Maybe their car was all their family had. I don't know what it's like to not have a home to return to; I do know that I tried to always say, "When you leave here today," rather than, "When you go home." A small gesture that I hoped would prevent the kids without homes from feeling isolated in their circumstance.

I ran what was called the Learning Center. Officially, young people could get help with their homework in that room and join prevention programs that measured how "successful" they were at avoiding drugs, sex, and ~~rock 'n' roll~~ the judicial system. Unofficially, it's where I had countless conversations with kids. Some of them were philosophers, speculating about existence: "How long the fish in that tank been waggin' its tail?" Others preached to their peers, "You gotta be gentle with the crayons. They didn't do nothing to you." Many possessed unfiltered honesty that I found so refreshing. When I was sitting with two six year old girls, helping them with their homework, one's face lit up and said, "Mmm! I smell some hamburgers." She assumed that's what was going to be served for dinner. The other girl deflated her excitement when she revealed, "That's my feet." She'd taken her jelly shoes off under the table and was swinging her legs back and forth. One of my absolute favorite things was to witness kids trying out a new word or phrase in a conversation. Sometimes slightly off the mark. I remember one time a six year old was deciding what song to sing for a talent show audition. He told me, "I need something that will really oppress the judges." It took me a minute to realize he meant "impress," but then when he decided to go with *O Canada*, I second guessed myself and wondered if maybe he was actually completely on point.

I loved the learning center and the freedom my supervisor gave me to make the space whatever I wanted it to be. I put an old fishing boat in it that had two swivel seats where kids could sit and read. And because I had no qualms about mixing boating references, I constructed a large canvas "sail" and painted on it, "Sail away into a book," meant to inspire kids to want to lose themselves in a story. I enlisted my 50 +1 CD player that once poured Air and Sean Lennon songs into my college dorm room to blast Backyardigans songs as kids arrived from school. Five minute dance parties were regular occurrences. The kids blew off steam from the day and I made it my mission to show them that not all adults take themselves seriously. We laughed together at our ridiculous dance moves. Most of the kids called me Megatron (my nickname) or Ms. Megatron (I loved when they called me this—they did so without pause, which made me feel like our time together was spent in a realm of magic realism). I watched kids grow from eager-to-please nine year olds, to brooding adolescents. I was invited to Quinceañeras, graduations, and baby showers.

Kids showed up to the center throughout the school year. Some found their way past the lure of computer screens in the technology lab and the excitement of the gym and joined the reading program that I ran in learning center. As I entered a new third grade girl's information into the reading program database, she stood next to me and watched. I filled various fields on the screen with pieces of data that would be matched with her comprehension quiz results, then aggregated with the other third graders in the program, and viewed in a report pulled by someone sitting in an office cubicle. They'd use that data to try and understand the girl standing next to me. They'd never actually look that girl in the eyes, or see how curious she was about the stories she read—the ones their software said she didn't comprehend.

This was when the girl tried to strike up a conversation by commenting on my "Chinese bangs." So young, yet already comfortable with the compliment opener. I wondered where she heard that term. I considered her Chinese bangs comment one that could reasonably be something she absorbed from the day-to-day exposure to American media. And it wasn't the first time a kid alluded to my ethnicity.

The kids I worked with forced me to face the Asian aspect of my identity in a way that I had never done so before. It felt like they were reaching out to connect with the part of me whose growth was stunted, that had never been cared for or developed. My parents and countless other parents of non-white adoptees were taught to take a color blind approach ("I don't see color," "I don't consider you *really* Asian/Black/Guatemalan...") to raising their kids. Unfortunately, denial of difference, denial of a kid's racial, ethnic, and transracial adoptee identities, means disempowerment of those parts of their selves. I remember being at the St. Louis Zoo on a humid summer day, my legs sticking to the wooden stroller my mom was pushing me around in. It matched all the other free strollers in the park. The oncoming strangers did double and triple takes, looking from my mom to me, and back at my mom. The confusion on their faces was familiar to me, it seemed to say, *something's off.* I had watched enough Sesame Street to know "which of these things is not like the others" in this scenario. I felt as watched and out of place as the polar bears nearby, clearly overheated as they lay belly up in the shallow pools of their manufactured habitat.

It's nearly impossible to understand something that's never talked about, especially for a kid. I sometimes wonder if I would have felt less embarrassment about looking different than my family if my parents had periodic conversations with me, ones where they'd acknowledge my ethnicity was different, and tell me that didn't prevent them from loving me.

One of the programs I developed and ran in the learning center was called Inner to Outer Beauty Salon. I'd sit with a group of six year olds as they each picked out a nail polish from the shoebox full of options that included Ruby Ruby and Rain Storm, Lacey Lilac and Celeb City. They sat and patiently participated in conversations, knowing my promise of painting their fingernails would follow. I started the program because I'd overheard some of the girls criticizing themselves, particularly the way they looked. I asked them questions like, "What makes you a good friend to others?" and "What is something amazing about you, that can't be seen just by looking at you?" I answered the questions with the girls, allowing me to benefit as well, from work that many people call "rewarding."

GUESSING GAMES

WITHIN FIVE MINUTES of arriving to a friend's wedding, a man walked up to me and said, "Are you Korean?" Just because I'm used to this type of abrupt interruption doesn't make it any more enjoyable. What I expect to be a celebratory occasion, honoring the partnership of two friends, is interrupted by this guy's need to involve me in his guessing game. The voice in my head goes agro and screams, WHAT THE FUCK DOES MY ETHNICITY MATTER IN YOUR EXPERIENCE OF THIS WEDDING? I WAS ENJOYING THIS MOMENT UNTIL YOU REMINDED ME THAT I STAND OUT FROM THE MAJORITY OF WHITE PEOPLE HERE. DO BETTER WITH YOUR CONVERSATION STARTER NEXT

TIME. My face detaches from all emotion when my mind rages like this, so the guy probably wondered why I suddenly looked blank and lifeless.

Life is not one giant game of Guess Who. I wouldn't be here if it was, and neither would any other Asian people because there isn't a single Asian person in the Hasbro board game. But I loved playing the 1982 edition of that game when I was a kid. At its best, it teaches kids deductive reasoning. At its worst, it subtly implies that if you're not a white man, you're at a disadvantage. So maybe it's more true to life than I realized? To play, each player randomly chooses a secret identity character card at the beginning of the game. To win, you must guess which character your opponent has before they guess yours; by asking questions that can be answered with "yes" or "no," you narrow down which character your competitor might have. Most of the characters were white guys. If the secret identity character card that you picked at the beginning of the game was David, Eric, Frans, or Paul, then you were in luck! Your chances of winning were good. However, if you got stuck with Claire, Maria, Peter, Robert, Susan, or Anne, your chances of winning were low. These are all mathematical facts (excuse me while I adjust my glasses), based on how many "distinct characteristics" each character had. At the time, I wasn't aware of the underlying lessons about power and privilege I was also absorbing.

There were only five female character cards in the set of 24, and I remember being disappointed every time I ended up with one of them. A female character weakened my position to win, and Anne— the only black character, was sure to deliver a loss. On occasion I did win with Anne, but I attribute that to playing with an adult who handed victories to kids. I didn't count those wins as real. But maybe I should have, because how is that win so different than a skill-less win made with David, who by the nature of his characteristics, puts a player at an advantage?

I can't say I love the feeling of winning. Even though I won Guess Who? as a kid by asking questions like, "Is your person a female?" and "Is your person black?" it's as if a seed of curiosity somewhere deep inside my mind spouted, "You won, but at what cost?" Looking back, I think just playing that game cost me pieces of my self-worth.

It might seem like such a small thing to some; it's just a game and so what if your chances of losing are greater if you pick a female character? But the feeling of disappointment that hit me every time it was revealed I picked a secret identity who was female sank to the bottom of my soul where it became an unrecognizable burden—a heckler who reminded me that I was a female, and therefore also a disappointment. I have wondered if I was a male, would my birth mom still have given me up? Probably. Or maybe not. I have no way of knowing. I can only guess.

One of my best childhood friends got married when we were in our 20's and I remember at her wedding reception, a group of us tried to guess which guy our very drunk friend was going to hook up with that night. We partied like we were still in college, like it was 1999, like we were so excited to be at the time in our lives when we were attending our own friend's wedding instead of one of our parents'.

Although playing the "who will hook up" game at weddings is entertaining, there are other opportunities for surmising. I've found myself wondering, "Who is crop dusting this cocktail and hors d'oeuvre hour?" and "Will there or won't there be a painfully inappropriate speech given tonight?" I wonder all of this to myself, and sometimes to a close friend or my date. I would never approach a stranger and say, "Excuse me, I've noticed there's an odor surrounding you, did you just fart?"

I survey the guy who asked me about my ethnicity and start to build a benefit of the doubt case for him. *At least he was specific and didn't ask the question I despise: "What are you?"* It's so vague and assumes I just know what's being asked. *Maybe he's just trying to connect through conversation and doesn't realize his topic of choice makes me feel reduced to my most obvious attribute.* Just as I finish telling myself the guy probably thinks he's making innocent small talk he says, "Yeah, you look *just* like my cousin's wife and she's Korean." Ah, the racist icing on the cake. You can try and scrape it off but it insists that all Asians *actually do* look alike.

Maybe this is why I prefer pie.

GAG ME WITH A CHOPSTICK

BEING ASIAN YET IDENTIFYING as white is common for adoptees raised in white families. I felt the tension created by this conundrum most when drunk men in bars would inquire, "You give massages with happy endings?" or catcall me on the street, as they sucked their teeth and crassly probed, "Sucky sucky?" All the privilege and comfort I grew up with disintegrated during these moments. I hated who and how the lesson came to me, but accepting the fact that I was an Asian American woman living in America was imperative.

Online dating for heteros in 2011 carried less of a stigma than in its earlier days, yet still managed to feel dehumanizing to me. My OkCupid profile explicitly stated, "I don't want to be contacted by dudes who have a 'thing' for Asians. I hated thinking about the assumptions—conscious and less so—guys made simply by looking at my profile picture. In some ways, dating felt like I was moonlighting as a myth buster who was tasked with debunking the fallacy that Asian women exist solely for the sexual fulfillment of men, that we are eager to please, that silence and submission are our definitive characteristics. On one particular date, the guy who sat across the table from me at a local tavern only seemed able to see me as a caricature of "Asian Woman" he'd pieced together from pop culture. He forced a conversation more unbearable than any of the bland and formulaic first date exchanges I'd had. I wanted to flip the fucking table.

***

Cats was the first show on Broadway that I ever saw. After my parents divorced, my dad began working for a company in NYC. Seeing Broadway shows became a thing we did when I visited. I was eleven when I was charmed and captivated by one of the *Cats* actors who sauntered up to where my dad and I were sitting in the Winter Garden Theater. During the overture, the actor began batting at the paper bag at my feet that I carried in from the Hard Rock Cafe. Not only did my first Broadway experience involve the fourth wall breaking, I felt *part* of the production. One of the actors touched my Hard Rock Cafe souvenir tee! I was fascinated by the grand, theatrical gesture of one of the cats rising up in the sky on a giant tire at the end of the show as horns played uplifting, tear-evoking music. I was so moved that when I returned to St. Louis, I recruited one of my best friends to "perform" *Cats* on roller skates with me in my basement as we blasted the soundtrack CD on my boombox. It was official, I was a fan of Broadway.

Miss Saigon is one play I never saw. It's as if I knew seeing it would be an assault on my developing adolescent sense of self. Despite hearing about an incredible moment involving a helicopter on stage, I stood firm and resisted going to see that play. I remember my dad asking if my avoidance of it was because it had to do with an Asian topic. I lied and said no.

The truth is I didn't have to see *Miss Saigon* to feel its effects. It was and still is part of our popular culture—that's what happens when you're one of the longest running shows on Broadway. The plot of *Miss Saigon* is based on Puccini's opera *Madame Butterly*, in which a Japanese geisha kills herself for a U.S. naval officer. *Miss Saigon* is set at the end of the Vietnam War. Chris, an American soldier, sees Kim, a new recruit to the Saigon brothel where he and his friends happen to be; Chris ends up "buying" Kim and her virginity, getting her pregnant, and abandoning her when he is deployed. Years pass and Kim is living in a shanty village with her two year old son, when Chris returns to Vietnam with his wife from America. Kim kills herself so Chris has to bring their child back to America.

Lyrics in the songs of *Miss Saigon* like "I'm gonna buy you a girl" and "The meat is cheap in Saigon" set a limited view of Vietnamese women. And because racism makes many people claim all Asians look alike, *Miss Saigon* reduces Asian women in general to exotic sex objects whose lives are worth so little that they sacrifice themselves so that their kids might have a shot at the American dream. I AM SO GLAD I NEVER CAME IN DIRECT CONTACT WITH THE NONSENSE THAT IS *MISS SAIGON*. My guess is that not many Asian people were ever in the audience. And I bet the mostly white audience members didn't have many if any Asian friends. So, whether we're aware of it or not, the racist and sexist, white savior narrative messages left an impression.

Misrepresentations of Asian women in pop culture extend well beyond Broadway. *Full Metal Jacket* came out in 1987 and although I never saw it, the line, "Me love you long time" spilled out of the mouths of men on the street and into my life, on numerous occasions. I don't watch *Law & Order: SVU*, but understand that the show routinely depicts Asian women as prostitutes and mail-order brides.

I find myself squirming in my seat when I hear about mail-order brides from Asia—the similarities of how adoptees and them end up in America doesn't escape me. The brides and I departed from a Confucian Society with little to offer girls and women that, let's be real, values us less than boys and men. We arrived in America where savior syndrome spreads the idea that we're better off in this sexist society than the one we came from. Expectations from the lives bought differ, but the dehumanizing price tag placed on a person sticks to them forever.

Ordering a wife like you might order a new gadget from Amazon is problematic to me. When slaves were bought, the people who paid believed they owned them. I sense men who buy mail-order brides must feel a similar sense of ownership, and when that power dynamic is in play, a relationship can never be a partnership.

When your first impression of someone is experienced through a screen, I think it takes some extra effort to get to know the real, unedited, nuanced version of them. So when I found myself on a first date and the guy started by asking me if my parents are citizens and moved on to assess how submissive I seem to be, I felt the rage inside me awaken. It's too exhausting to recognize what the rage really is—the hurt and fury that's an accumulation of all the racist microaggressions I've experienced or been exposed to in my life, so I contain it. I tell myself it's for my own good, for self-preservation. Funny how destruction has the ability to disguise itself. I want to flip the fucking table. I don't flip the table. As much as I'd like to hate the player, I know he's just a piece in the game.

TOUCHING THE VOID

VANILLA LONG JOHN WAS the go-to donut of my childhood. Anything with sprinkles on it or jelly in it just seemed like too much of a mess. Donut holes were appealing to me, but I couldn't get over how inaccurate their name felt. They seemed more plug-ish than hole-ish. If they *were* called donut plugs I might have fully embraced them, thinking they could patch up the cracks in my heart.

Some hearts break into pieces over the span of many years. Mine was cracked wide open when my birth mom relinquished me—when I was cut off from my Korean bloodline and became a statistic in Korea's growing adoptee demographic (I was one of about 2,000 babies exported from the country in

1981). I have no actual memory of the moment of separation from the woman who carried me in her womb, but it did leave me with a souvenir of sorts when I was growing up—a voraciousness that aimed itself at food.

There's a difference between enjoying the taste of food, eating what your body needs for nutrients, and seeking comfort from the pleasure of its taste by devouring all sweet and salty snacks within reach. I'm fortunate that I made myself sick only once from eating too much. I was about 11 years old on a family vacation to Disney World with my dad, stepmom, and baby stepbrother. We were staying in a suite that had a kitchen where we could cook our own meals. I don't remember what dinner was, likely two generous servings of sloppy joe's and mashed potatoes. I was swept up in the idea that Disney World was the happiest place on earth, and took it upon myself to comfort eat my way into a state of rapture. The thing that pushed me over the edge from ecstasy to misery, though, were blueberry Eggo waffles I ate for dessert. Not an item that ever found its way onto the grocery list at my house where I lived with my mom, the bright yellow box with bold, red, rounded lettering that read "Eggo" called to me. *Megan, you're on VACATION. Treat yourself. You want us. You want to toast us to perfection so there's just a little browning on our edges, and then you want to spread butter all over us and hold us in your hand as you bite into processed perfection.*

When I rose from bed later that night and puked into the toilet, remnants of those blueberry waffles floated on the surface, reminders of my overindulgence, bile beacons warning that I'd had too much. Ashamed to tell my dad or stepmom what happened, I stood alone in the bathroom and felt scared when I realized my body was sending me a message: it literally refused to accept this method of fulfillment. When I flushed away the partially digested contents evicted from my stomach, I told myself *never again.*

Alcohol is not food, so technically I kept my promise. But really I just created a loophole that made way for my voraciousness to reach the fun and dangerous vice of my twenties. Like food, booze provided the illusion of wholeness and urged me to keep consuming. Better than food, alcohol transformed me into the most extroverted version of myself. And we live in an extrovert's world, so to be an extroverted girl and fit in felt amazing. I made friends through the simple act of drinking. I joined the women's rugby team at my college; we drank boxed wine at practice on Fridays and I drank vodka at our parties like it was water—the team bought me my first flask. It was inscribed with my nickname, "Megatron."

If I wasn't pulling from my flask, I was drinking something stiff from the 52oz "Super Big Gulp Plus" mug gifted to me by a dorm-mate. My nickname was written on that vessel as well in black permanent marker. Apparently, I was possessive of my spirits—they were liquid courage and I didn't want to lose them. I drank a lot. People asked me, "Where does it all go?"

***

Meramec Caverns was one of the most fascinating field trips I went on in elementary school. There's 4.6 miles of hollow space underground, formed over millions of years by the erosion of limestone. I remember walking through the dimly lit caves, gazing at stalactites hanging from above, amazed at how the air felt against my hands when I slowly waved them in front of me. At one point during the guided tour, we were told to stop walking and be very still. The guide turned off all the lights and my entire class was swallowed by darkness. My eyes were open but I could not see. I sensed the vastness of the cave system while my imagination scanned toward the surface; it created for me visions of people in broad daylight, unaware of the dark hollow beneath the earth's surface.

I don't think the people who saw me drink ludicrous amounts of liquor were aware of a similar hollow, cave-like part of my heart, let alone its expanse. There's no way. That's why they wondered, "Where does it all go?" They were only acquainted with my voraciousness, which eagerly consumed a variety of spirits, none of which were ever able to fill the emptiness inside.

The Eggo waffle realization of my drinking days came during a text session with a friend, long after I'd graduated from college. I had been blackout drunk the previous night and she was checking in on me to make sure I was okay. When I asked her if she caught the name of the guy who took me home and stayed the night, she was shocked to find out he was a stranger. We joked about it. I ended up referring to him as "the boy scout" because he was totally prepared for a sleepover—change of clothes and contact solution in his bag. Keeping our text-versation light and laughing about it delayed the severity of the situation from settling.

I consider myself a feminist. I value women as a reminder to value myself. I point out double standards and the invisibility of women in the workplace. I am a beneficiary of the sexual revolution and a disciple of *Sex and the City*. I'm confident about the choices I've made about birth control and sexual behavior—for the most part. But not that night with the guy whose name I do not know. That night crossed the line from no strings attached sexual libration, to sheer recklessness. How do you give consent when you're blacked out? You don't. Legally, consent can't even happen under the influence of alcohol or drugs. I don't remember force or violence. I don't remember intercourse. I don't remember wanting or not wanting. Maybe the open condom wrappers I found scattered throughout my apartment were all false starts. I don't remember.

I blankly stared at my phone's screen. The absence of memories reminded me too much of the hollowness I was trying to *fill* with alcohol. My consumption had turned on me, the cavernous space in my heart expanded.

My unsuccessful attempts to fill the vacancy inside me continued. Food and booze remained in the mix, joined by long lists of tasks titled "To Do." Retail therapy never appealed to me, probably because it had the word "therapy" in it. I found comfort in connecting with a group of friends who were all engaged in various creative projects. We started meeting on a regular basis; we were a mix of artists, entrepreneurs, and writers. There was an air of expectancy when we met, each of us delivered stories or ideas that were received with open arms. One offspring of this collective was the summer of OOB (out of the box).

OOB was about treating our lives as important expressions of our creativity. For the single people in the group, this meant using dating to reveal our personalities. Instead of sitting through banal conversation just because that's what we'd come to expect from first dates, we planned parkour picnics on rooftops and triple dates unlocked by solving a cipher. That last idea was mine and an attempt to woo a mathematician. It worked really well with a swiftness I wasn't exactly prepared for.

We spent zero dates in the superficial realm of conversation and dove deep to the mathematician's feelings about his newly divorced parents. I found his openness and insistence on being vulnerable both refreshing and terrifying; he talked unabashedly about the things that caused cracks in his own heart. He was soft-spoken and sensitive. I quickly learned there was much more to Kagen than the "math genius" label given to him.

Kagen asked me, "How do you feel?" a lot. I wasn't great at giving emotional responses. It was challenging for me to answer him with more than "good" or "bad" without accessing my heart, which I hadn't practiced much in my life. I don't remember my family being the type to talk about feelings. We were more of the TCB variety. For you non-TCB folks who grew up in families that sat around expressing your feelings to each other, TCB stands for TAKING CARE OF BUSINESS. My family was a crew of DOERS. We set goals and achieved them by making a plan and activating hard work ethic, a value in our tribe, that trumped anything that resembled processing or expressing feelings.

Sometimes I wonder why I wasn't asked to express what I was feeling. Was it because…I was adopted? Were my parents protecting me from sliding down the slippery slope of emotions and ending up in the expansive landscape of alternate realities? *If I stayed in Korea, would I be an orphan or living on the street? What would that feel like? If I ended up with one of the other two families whose adoptees traveled over from Korea with me on the plane, what would living in rural Missouri be like? Does my homegrown older brother wish that I never showed up so he could have our parents to himself?* My wondering led me to face the blank space where my origin story belonged.

Although my parents had conversations with me about how I was adopted, it wasn't terrain we navigated very often. I was told we were a family. We were. But at the same time, we weren't like the family next door. We weren't even like the family down the street. And yet, looking back on it, I think we tried to fit the mold. We did little reinventing and mostly just pretended like me being relinquished by my biological mother on the other side of the world was no biggie. *Gaping hole in my heart from abandonment, what? Where? I don't see it. It must not be there.* "Out of sight, out of mind" is a catchy phrase, but it fails to consider the heart and its desires.

I didn't tread lightly when it came to feeling emotions—even that proximity felt dangerous. I stayed mostly in my head, except Kagen insisted I toe the line if our relationship was to move forward. For the first time ever, I Googled "psychological issues of Korean adoptees." Reading the accounts of other adoptees was rough. It was like I was reading my own story; I was shaken out of the denial I'd lived in my entire life about what it means—what it feels like—to be an adoptee. Apparently adoptive parents were commonly coached to tell their kids that they were "chosen." I definitely remember feeling good when my mom told me that because it balanced out kids' remarks about how I was given up for adoption because nobody wanted me. However, the article added that being a "chosen one" could cause adoptees to feel like they have to prove that they deserve their place in the family. Even though I wasn't afraid of being kicked out of my family for failure to make my bed, some level of concern breached my consciousness from hearing friends taunt their younger siblings with the threat, "If you don't behave, mom and dad are going to put you up for adoption!"

The article online also mentioned that for an adoptee, loss, along with feelings of rejection, shame, and grief, might impede the development of intimacy. "One maladaptive way to avoid possible reenactment of previous losses is to avoid closeness and commitment." I found it difficult to accept that a single event so early on in my life could have such an impact on me. Admitting that I'd been avoiding intimacy was a real blow to the ego. It felt like surrender; like the armor disguised as independence and self-sufficiency was falling apart. It's such a mind fuck to realize that what you thought was a means of protection is also a mechanism of isolation.

When you're attempting to pick up the pieces of your mind after it's been blown, it's nice to have a professional around. Kagen suggested we go see a therapist together, because in addition to the minor identity crisis I was going through, we'd recently decided to live together. Kagen and Cube—the cat that came with him—moved into the 800 square foot apartment I'd lived in on my own for the past seven years. My reaction was similar to what I imagine it looks like when you introduce new inhabitants to any established habitat—animalistic. My turf was no longer my own. I battled with Cube by refusing to let him into the bedroom area, which didn't work because cats always get what they want. Cube hissed at me and I tried sweeping him out from under the bed with a broom. Cleaning and keeping the apartment tidy became the focal point of my voraciousness. Instead of talking to Kagen about feeling like I was losing the single, fabulous, independent part of myself, I just kept cleaning— until the day he brought me to go see Barbara for couples counseling.

Still within the range of denial's grasp, I remember getting to Barbara's office before Kagen for our first session. I sat on her couch and told her, "This is something Kagen wants to do, so I'm here for him." However, it didn't take long for me to benefit from the therapy and understand how crucial it was to build the type of relationship Kagen and I wanted to be in. It took a lot longer for me to realize the enormity of therapy's impact. One of the books Barbara recommended we read was *Hold Me Tight* by Dr. Sue Johnson. It's based on Emotionally Focused Therapy (EFT); Dr. Johnson explains EFT's message in the introduction:

> Forget about learning how to argue better, analyzing your early childhood, making grand romantic gestures, or experimenting with new sexual positions. Instead, recognize and admit that you are emotionally attached to and dependent on your partner in much the same way that a child is on a parent for nurturing, soothing, and protection. Adult attachments may be more reciprocal and less centered on physical contact, but the nature of the emotional bond is the same. EFT focuses on creating and strengthening this emotional bond between partners by identifying and transforming the key moments that foster an adult loving relationship: being open, attuned, and responsive to each other.

Attachment. It's as simple as adding a document to an email, and as complex as a single broken bond that hinders one's ability to trust in the durability of all future relationships. For some, the break comes when their first pet dies, or with the death of a parent. For me, the break came shortly after birth, so when the emotional bond between Kagen and I developed, I could see how I'd been unwilling to attach emotionally to anyone, ever. I felt sad and guilty when I began to understand what was missing from my relationships with my parents, brothers, and previous partners. It took time to reconcile the *what if I could have emotionally attached to...* scenarios of my past.

When Kagen and I got married, our emotional attachment was solid, but still strengthening. We promised to prioritize our bond to each other, which requires work. And more work. And then when we think we're in the clear, happily ever after on the horizon—more work. A lot of times the work involves a simple hug when instinct tells me I need space. This is a lot harder to do than it sounds. Going in for a hug is the last thing I want to do when my feelings are hurt or I'm feeling guarded, but it's the exact action that has the power to reconnect Kagen and me during discordant moments. Our bond has become strong enough that it keeps me tethered to the surface where there is light, so I can safely explore the dark hollow of my heart, and begin to make some repairs.

NAME CHANGER

I ACCIDENTALLY BUMPED into a woman at the grocery store. She looked at me with angry eyes and spit, "Gook!" Every muscle tensed, my body rigid and prepared to deflect any additional racial slurs hurled at me. None came. The woman walked away casually pushing her cart, and my mind defaulted to the question planted in me a decade earlier, courtesy of Shakespeare and my favorite high school English teacher: *What's in a name?* It pokes holes in the label "gook" but all the feelings the term evokes linger.

Names matter. They frame how we see ourselves and others. Quicke (silent e), my last name when I was growing up, tended to throw people off if they didn't know I was adopted. I remember once when I was in high school I went to my boyfriend's house after school. He was multiracial, his mom was

Asian and his dad was white. His grandma was on the phone on speaker, and we were in the kitchen as my boyfriend fielded her interrogation about the validity of my Asianess. "Quicke? That's not Asian," she drilled.

His face blushed slightly as it became evident he'd already told her about me and that I was Asian. He replied, "Well, she is."

"Quicke? What kind of name is that?" she huffed.

In that moment, I felt like an imposter. Technically yes, I was Asian. But not the type of Asian that my boyfriend's grandma would be pleased for her grandson to be dating. I sensed he was excited to tell her the girl he was dating was Asian, but didn't think about the degrees of Asianness to be considered.

For a long time I clung to *What's in a name?* as if it were a solid rebuttal rather than a prompt to ponder and explore. I read that line *What's in a name? That which we call a rose/By any other word would smell as sweet* hundreds of times when I had to memorize lines from *Romeo and Juliet* for English class. I interpreted *What's in a name?* to essentially mean, "Eh, names are no biggie," which was convenient, seeing how I spelled my last name incorrectly for the majority of my school career. The story goes, my first grade teacher thought it would be easier on me to be "Megan Quick" rather than "Megan Quicke," which was sure to invite unwanted taunting of "Hey quickie!" Looking back, I'm doubtful that's really how it all went down. I suspect my mom, who'd lived with the name "Quicke" for most of her adult life, was being overprotective and took action to prevent me from having to engage with the dirty joke, "Are you a quickie?" When I did put the 'e' back on my last name, it wasn't long before friends started calling me "Quick-e." They had already given me plenty of other nicknames (quickster, Nestle quick, quick stop, DJ quik…) so it didn't offend me, I considered it just another spin on my last name that I loved.

Nicknames are fun. I've acquired numerous ones throughout my life, some lasting days, others decades. There's one that channeled more love than the rest, it's the one that was given to me my first year in college by a friend and I used years later when I was a camp counselor: Megatron. Every time I'd hear campers shout, "Megatron!" to get my attention, my heart swelled from the joy in their voices. My campers fully bought into my nickname, which made me feel like I was living in a magical, parallel reality, where I was as amazing as they believed me to be. My options as Megatron seemed limitless, the name itself had so much room in it and allowed me to be many things.

The same can't be said for all names, or their close relative, labels. It's amazing to me how quickly certain designations can strip people of their dignity. Without realizing it, we start seeing the label instead of the person: disabled, low-income, ADHD. Sometimes we pigeonhole ourselves: "I'm a dog person." "I'm a cat person." As if loving both is a betrayal to one or the other.

Terms for minority groups in America that were once widely accepted have been revised. Sometimes for accuracy, sometimes for kindness. Both are valid. People who are fully able bodied probably spend little time thinking about the difference between the terms "disabled," "differently abled," and the crude term that begins with "R" that was widely used not so long ago. Similarly, European

Americans may not wonder why the explanatory prefix was dropped from their identity, yet remains for other Americans who came from Africa or Asia.

Names are negotiable. When my soon to be husband (a term whose historical meaning doesn't escape me; I sometimes replace with "partner" but I'm still searching for a label that feels like a better fit) and I were about to get married, we decided to change our last names in a non-traditional way. For us, me taking his last name felt antiquated, and combining them made for a mouthful of mishmash. We narrowed down the possibilities by linking our new, chosen last name to our occupations. My partner makes structurally sound puzzle boxes and mechanical furniture and my work includes offering sound advice to individuals. Sound felt like a name we could grow into together.

And we have. Turns out there's a lot to the name Sound. I like considering some of the synonyms as aspirational characteristics to strive for: healthy, reliable, sagacious, peaceful, secure. I encountered someone whose first impression of the name reminded them of whales and the number of waterways near where they grew up. A few people have told me how cool it would be if I were a DJ. My guess is that some people might recall the phrase "safe and sound" when they hear the name. Or maybe they remember a sound sleep they recently had. It's all relative. There's a staff member at the local garden shop I go to who has asked me about my last name. On one of my visits when she was working, she told me that she shared with her partner the story of how Kagen and I chose our last name and said they liked that approach so much they planned to do the same.

A metal plaque that my mom gave us hangs next to our front door and greets every visitor to our home, "Sound Space Est. May 29, 2014." More than our initial intention of reflecting our occupations, Sound has come to define our living space as well—a peaceful oasis, a reliable place for us to continue designing our lives in a way that feels meaningful and progressive. Names matter. They frame how we see ourselves and others. I don't know which comes first, changing minds or changing labels. I'm dedicated to doing both.

TO BREED, OR NOT TO BREED

THE SINGLE BIT OF INFORMATION I know about my birth mom—that she was fertile enough to have me—led me to believe I'd have no problem getting pregnant. I was wrong.

I felt I was on the cusp of pregnancy when my doctor removed my IUD. She said, "You're officially able to get pregnant." Looking back, I think she said this to make sure I knew that removing the copper device from my uterus meant its effect of preventing pregnancy was immediately gone (a rumor I'd heard was that it takes a few months for the reproductive system to be fully functional after an IUD removal). I had no way of knowing that I was far from the cusp of pregnancy, that the process of trying to get pregnant would force me to consider my identity as an adoptee, or that my husband Kagen and I were actually about to enter years of what we'd eventually come to call pregatory—a place full of uncertainty where thoughts about fertility hijack the mind constantly, where it's unclear whether choices are something you make or are actually just decisions you're driven to by circumstance.

I was on the pill long before it was necessary. At seventeen, my mom told me it would be good for my complexion, but the timing of her concern for my teenage pimples curiously coincided with me starting to date a guy. Teenage pregnancy wasn't common at my high school, at least not the kind that was carried to term. I knew of one teen mom; the behind the back judgement I heard whispered about her was enough to keep me ten steps away from ever following in my biological mother's footsteps and becoming an unwed mother.

Nearly two decades and several "do we want to have a kid?" conversations later, Kagen and I entered the world of trying to conceive (TTC for short because it's less exhausting than repeating t r y i n g   t o   c o n c e i v e over and over and over and over again). By a year in to TTC, I was aware of every pregnant woman around me. It's like when you decide you want to buy a certain car, and then you start noticing that same car model everywhere. One day when I was sitting at my desk at work, a coworker who I wasn't particularly a fan of stopped by for her daily gossip session with someone seated near me. She was about a trimester into her second pregnancy and I overheard her say, "We totally weren't expecting this one. Oops!" Everything I mildly disliked about this woman suddenly amplified in my mind; noxious thoughts solidified into sentences I imagined hurling at her.

Spending an extended amount of time in pregatory and TTC is humbling. I consider myself an intellectual, an open-minded evolved being, and a feminist who practices values and doesn't just pay them lip service. To be faced with the inability to get pregnant made me question my worth as a woman and myself for caring so much that I couldn't. Determination and desperation got muddled up in my mind.

After two years of TTC, a fertility specialist diagnosed Kagen and me with "unexplained infertility." His sperm analysis came back normal and all the tests I took indicated that my entire reproduction system was in quality working order. So I ventured outside of Western medicine and explored the world of alternative medicine, thinking maybe what went unexplained in one sphere could be clarified in another.

The bridge was acupuncture. My OBGYN had mentioned that there were studies showing acupuncture treatments could improve hormone production needed for a healthy menstrual cycle, and in turn, a healthy pregnancy. I visited an amazing acupuncturist who specialized in fertility, but the cost and time to drive to her office eventually prohibited me from seeing her. A friend told me about a community acupuncture center that had a sliding scale for payment, so I began going there. After five months of being treated by various acupuncturists, the one who did my initial intake paperwork and who I got a strong "I'm going to fix this" vibe from seemed perplexed that I had not yet conceived. She drilled me with the standard line of questioning: *Have you tested your hormone levels?*

Did you have an ultrasound done to make sure your fallopian tubes aren't blocked? Have you had your eggs tested? Has your husband's sperm been tested? Are you eating healthily and exercising regularly? All yes, yet the questioning managed to make me doubt myself. Was I missing something, was there more I could do? I started to try treatments that felt like I might as well visit a magician and ask them to abracadabra a fetus into my womb. It wasn't exactly clear what a Mayan abdominal massage might do for me or my chances of getting pregnant, but I ended up following through with that recommendation given to me by one of the acupuncturists. The masseuse suggested I try a castor oil pack, which I *think* was believed to help the function of my lymphatic system.

Another suggestion from the masseuse led me to buying a cellophane bag filled with yarrow, calendula, rose, rosemary, and basil. It crumpled in my hand as I turned it to read the instructions.

> *Uterine Steam: Crush the herbs into a pot of hot water thanking them for helping with your healing. Offer a prayer nine times to whomever offers you spiritual guidance; Universal Energy, Jesus Christ, God, Goddess, Mother Earth, etc. It is the prayer*

and the intention that is important. Bring this to a soft boil for 10 minutes, steep for 5 minutes with the lid on. Place the pot under a chair or stool with large enough opening in the center. Sit down without underwear, but wearing socks. Drape a blanket all around you fully to the floor. Be careful not to allow any draft underneath you. Sit quietly over your pot of herbal steam for 20 minutes.

Half an hour later I was convinced it wouldn't work because I wasn't enough of a believer.

My outlook each month was cyclical: ready/focused/optimistic, excited/hopeful/expectant, disappointed/empty/discouraged. Rinse and repeat. Some people can keep going through this routine like the Energizer Bunny. For others, it's straight to the most promising medical fertility method like taking Clomid, paired with an assist from a specialist; like Intrauterine insemination (the strongest, best swimming, most determined sperm are identified in a lab and injected into the uterus, fingers crossed they reach the fallopian tubes, where fertilization occurs); or In Vitro Fertilization (an egg is removed from the ovary and combined in a lab dish with strong, determined sperm; the embryo is inserted into the uterus with hopes of implantation). Kagen and I chose to pause at this crossroads. Moving forward down the medicalized path felt impatient. Even though we'd been TTC for nearly three years, we had several more years until I turned 40, the milestone we'd talked about as the logical time to intentionally stop TTC, due to the increased chance of complications and genetic diseases. We were sad, but resolved, to end our efforts of t r y i n g   t o   c o n c e i v e .

Making peace with something doesn't necessarily mean keeping the peace is a given. There's a popular urban myth about couples who get pregnant the moment they stop trying that paid my consciousness a visit on a number of occasions. Then one day about a year later it stopped. I began to imagine what Kagen and my future life might look like without kids. We'd have to intentionally decide where and how to direct the reserve of love we weren't spending on offspring. Some might struggle with being in this position of self-invention. *Where do you begin to build when the plan you had isn't viable? How do you know what the right decisions are?* I realized my experience as an adoptee, as someone who has a blank space of unknown at the very beginning of my life, makes me familiar with the necessity of self-invention and comfortable with being the one who blurs the lines that define: who are we, why are we here, what's our purpose?

For my birth mom, sending me overseas was viewed as the best option in a society that was prejudiced against single mothers, unwelcoming for kids born outside marriage, and shunned domestic adoptions. What choice did she actually have?

By the time I became pregnant, it felt less like an active choice and more like a video I'd been waiting to stream online finally finished buffering. The subtle ways in which I felt different leading up to the day I was supposed to get my period were so little and so late to the TTC party, I barely acknowledged them. But they were enough of a blip to cause me to dig out a pregnancy test from the linen closet. It was old and about to expire. I peed on it. In less than a minute, the positive blue sign appeared.

I proceeded through the first trimester with caution, knowing that at my age, the risk of miscarriage was higher than if Kagen and I were expectant parents when we first started TTC four years earlier. One of the books I checked out from the library suggested I ask my mother to tell me her story of giving birth to me. *What does your mother remember about going into labor? What did your father do? What did her caregivers do and say? What did she feel when she first saw you and held you? How does your mother feel now about your birth?* I'm not sure if my birth mother held me after I was born. The stories of that day, her pregnancy with me, and her feelings about it all, are lost to me.

I imagine that when my daughter is old enough, I will delight in telling her all the details about when I first felt her move around in the womb, how excited I was to meet her, and how when their dad and I brought her home from the hospital, all we could do was stare at her in awe. She'll hear about how excited our friends and family were when we shared the news of her existence; I'll tell her how my favorite reactions were the verbal bursts of emotion and reenact each one, ad nauseam. My child will have no choice. She'll be bombarded with stories.

MESSAGE IN A BOTTLE TO MY BIRTH MOM

Dear Birth Mother,

I hope you're not insulted by the greeting I chose. I looked up "Korean honorifics" on the internet because I want to show you respect, but I'm filled with uncertainty when it comes to Korean values, language, and traditions. I'm not sure which option is the most appropriate for our particular relationship. Also, I don't expect you'll ever actually read this, because that's how messages in bottles work. I'm sending this out to sea, with hopes that its spirit will reach you and you'll somehow feel I'm thinking of you. Sounds magical and sentimental and doubtful all at the same time, doesn't it?

When I was young, my understanding of where I came from was fuzzy and relied on my mom's best guess, based on the information given to her by the adoption agency. She told me you were a 20-year-old unmarried woman, who wrote to the Korean man in the military who was (biologically speaking) half the cause of me being born, to see if he would marry you and start a family. I'm told he never responded. The characters in this account lack depth and complexity, and for a long time it was difficult for me to understand that you were an actual human being. This, paired with "If you grew up in Korea, you probably…" stories were enough to make me feel fortunate to be part of the family I was placed in. Being grateful for what I had meant not questioning what I was without.

My gratitude couldn't transform my family to become what I learned a family is supposed to look like—compliments of every family tree activity I ever had to do in school. I've heard teachers try to make it more inclusive now, but when I was required to complete family tree assignments, value and emphasis were placed on bloodline. Clearly, I was doing it wrong and had no means to make it right. I felt so much shame about that. I wonder if there is a space with my name on your version of a family tree, or if you feel too much shame yourself to make it so?

I thought about you very little for a long time, then I thought about you a lot during the spring of my junior year in college. I felt my sudden interest was a sign. I thought maybe you died and your spirit visited me, because you wanted to make sure I didn't forget you. Was I right? Was that you? Is it you with me when the leaves rustle in the wind and I am reminded that everything is interconnected? Is it you who led me to Kagen, because you knew the scars on my soul from my separation from you could finally heal from being near his kindness and sensitivity? Did you know that his love would keep me from falling to pieces when I read that article in *The New York Times Magazine* about Korean adoptees?

I remember feeling ridiculous, to be over 30 years old and for the first time, questioning a significant piece of my history: My creation story. Was it true? Did it omit important information about you that could help me better understand your choice to give me away? The *Times* article was comprehensive. It covered the political factors that led to the development of Korea's adoption industry and the personal journeys of a handful of adoptees who have moved to Korea and live among hundreds of adoptees. I was comforted and troubled by the familiarity I found:

> *In a 2009 survey of adult adoptees by the Donaldson Adoption Institute, more than 75 percent of the 179 Korean respondents who grew up with two white parents said they thought of themselves as white or wanted to be white when they were children...*
>
> *Eleana Kim, the author of "Adopted Territory," says it's a common anxiety among adoptees who often dread "coming out" to their parents—whether it's in the form of birth-family searches, returning to birth countries or criticizing the adoption system...*
>
> *For many adoptees, those cultural divides— coupled with the fact that they can't speak the language, a frustrating and often heart-wrenching obstacle in their own birth country—solidifies the feeling that they hover in between: not fully American, not fully Korean...*

There were questions raised that I wondered too (should adopted children be brought up by people of a different race?); points resonated—feelings I'd had but never made real with words: *But while the predominant narrative of adoption focuses on what is gained, each adoption also entails loss for both the child and her biological family.*

Adjusting the frame I looked at my adoption through, seeing it as a loss as well as a gain, was deeply painful. I don't know how else to say it. I was raised to focus on the positive. This perspective is nice but not always true. Recognizing my adoption as a loss as well as a gain felt honest. More honesty followed. I realized I could love and care for my family AND be interested in my Korean heritage.

I want you to know I'm not angry with you. I don't have enough information to make that call and even if I did, the Buddhist in me defaults to forgiveness and compassion. I'm not sure if you're of a certain faith, but I like to imagine my gravitation toward Buddhism is because of you, or the generations that proceeded us. My introduction took place in academia (I majored in religion in college), I practice every day in a small ways that impact my life greatly.

There's a lot about you that I'll never know. Like if we share facial expressions or mannerisms (these may be learned things but I like imagining I at least have your eyes). You will forever be a mystery to me, you're my ultimate teacher in acceptance of the unknown. Even if I could know you, knowledge doesn't undo the feeling of being incomplete that followed me around for all those years I tried stuffing myself with busyness and accomplishments.

At some relatively recent point, I accepted that I was relinquished by you when I was a baby. I don't know if you held me or ever loved me—I've accepted these things too. There's a beautiful song written by a woman named Stevie Nicks that brings me to tears every time I hear it. Some of its lyrics capture the stuck space I was in before I accepted that I'll never know you.

Well, I've been afraid of changin'
'Cause I've built my life around you
But time makes you bolder
Even children get older
And I'm getting older, too

Without fully realizing it, I think my sense of self formed around the significant space of the unknown of you. I wasn't able to expand after a certain point because the big empty space was a placeholder for you. A hopeless romantic of a whisper suggested that maybe one day I'd meet you. This visitor was well-intentioned, yet misinformed.

I want you to know why I will not search for you. It's a combination of things, really. As I mentioned, I feel like you may have already passed from this life, journeyed to the other side of the mountain. In this case, searching for you would be superfluous. Sometimes I wonder if my logical way of thinking through a problem comes from you. If we are wired the same in that way, I think you'll understand my decision without hurt feelings. Mostly though, I don't have to meet you, see you, talk to you, to know that I came from you. I've spent hours in reflection and realized collecting facts and information is unnecessary for me to be at peace.

Sometimes I wonder if you are calm in your heart. I hope you are, and that wherever you are—in this life or the next—this message of mine reaches you. Maybe it will be carried to you by the wind and

when you feel the breeze on your skin you'll know
I'm thinking of you.

Thank you for bringing me into this world.
A piece of my heart will always belong to you.
Megan (Um Mee Ja)

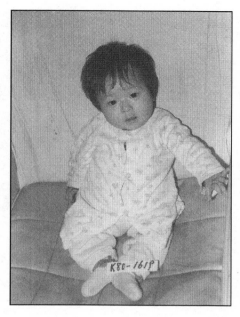

Um Mee Ja aka Megan aka Baby Megatron

This is the photo my parents were given before my arrival to the United States.

I learned how to use chopsticks the way suburban kids
did —like tweezers.

Margaret Cho gives great hugs, which was especially nice since I couldn't stop crying when I met her.

Meet Cube, who won my heart and made me a cat convert. So much so that when Kagen and I attended a cat and dog themed party, I proudly and geekily proclaimed my allegiance to felines.

ACKNOWLEDGMENTS

Ready or not, here comes another story: I did not want to write this book. I wanted to write a book about coffee and all its parallels to human development. I raised money to explore the coffee industry and interview individuals like Piero Bambi. I fell down a rabbit hole (an extremely caffeinated one, at that) and in many ways, got lost in the creative process. For seven years. There's a lot I can say about THE CREATIVE PROCESS and why I chose not to write a book about coffee, but I won't. Because I know some of you would just roll your eyes and judge the shit outta what might come off as "hippy dippy new age magical thinking." Also, maybe I'll write a book about the creative process one day and then the haters won't have to read it, the rest of you can. All that to say, there are some people who supported my idea of that book about coffee that transformed into this much more personal book about identity. I see the two as connected and hope these individuals aren't too disappointed that the project they backed took a hard pivot. Thanks for supporting the creative process: Izaiah Buseth, Stephen Malloy Brackett, Andrew Guerrero, John & Nancy Quicke, Alex & Barbara Burgard, Gail Marie, Mitch Morgan, Ryan Kelley, Mark Overly, Dan Bush, Erin Rollman, Jan & Jim Leuthauser, Brenda Uhler, Melissa Harris, Nick McGrane, Marc Hughes, Rick Cope, Peter Swenson, Nathan Quicke, Lori Thompson, Karyn Bocko, and Ariah Gamaldi.

There are many people I could thank, because I'm a HUGE fan of gratitude. However, I want to focus on the people who specifically helped me bring this book into the world. Thanks to Jason and Kalen who were generous with their time and insight into the publishing industry. Thanks to Eleanor, my editor and friend whose encouragement at the end of this whole process was a welcome final push of motivation. Thanks to Bird, who read and gave feedback when the essays were nothing more than vignettes.

Thanks to Kagen for infinite patience, compassionate encouragement, and unconditional love. |#|

Made in the USA
San Bernardino, CA
27 February 2018